Wild Food Foraging in Devon

Rachel Lambert

Pocket Devon

TOR MARK

Alison Hodge is an imprint of Tor Mark Ltd,
United Downs Industrial Estate, St Day,
Redruth, Cornwall TR16 5HY

Published 2023

www.tormark.co.uk

ISBN 9780 85025 803 5

Printed and bound in the UK

As with all cultivated foods, wild foods can cause an allergic reaction in some people. Brief medicinal uses are given within plant descriptions for interest, including plants to avoid when pregnant (carrot seeds) and common allergens (celery and mustard). However, this is not a plant medicine guide and medical advice should be sought if you have a specific health condition or concern. Please adhere to all guidance given and take responsibility for your own choices. Always be 100% certain of a plant before tasting and seek guidance from an expert.

 Printed on FSC Mix

CONTENTS

INTRODUCTION

It was here in Devon, almost 30 years ago, that I first became aware of the abundance of wild food and medicine surrounding us. I was walking along a typical footpath with two friends, when Martin stopped by a stone-wall and showed me Pennywort (page 74) growing out of the cracks. 'You can eat that', he said handing me one, and my world changed forever.

As a child, I may have eaten my weight in blackberries, but I was oblivious to the fact that so many more of the trees, weeds and foliage around me were edible. Of course, the next question is which are edible and are they tasty or good for you? This starting point sent me on a journey of discovery, meeting knowledgeable teachers, nature-loving elders (I was in my early twenties at the time) and making new friends who generously shared facts and understanding so I could learn how to forage safely. The pleasure of spending time in nature and simply gathering her bounty still brings a smile to my face. Sharing this information and ancient wisdom with you increases that joy.

Rachel x

FORAGING IN DEVON

The foraging potential of such a vast county is hard to condense into a small, pocket book. My inspiration comes from the fact that Devon has more roads than any county in the UK (think winding, narrow tracks to major A roads), it reaches the coast on both the north and south, has characteristic stone-walls and hedges plus wonderful moorland and open-wilderness contained within these boundaries. Devon also goes from sea-level to High Willyways (also known as High Willies) on Dartmoor at 621 metres, giving a wide range of terrains and growing environments for flora to prosper.

In this book I share 18 of my favourite wild foods from the hedges, rural roadsides, rivers, coast, old field systems, grassland, gardens and woodlands of Devon. In this beautiful and diverse county I cover a range of plants that flourish here. None of the forageable foods covered are rare or protected, yet all still demand our respect and considered picking. The generosity of nature is to be valued, especially as our relationship with planet earth becomes more fragile as a result of our human impact and climate change.

I have omitted mushrooms and fungi, not because they are not worthy, but because their potential is beyond the scope of this book and they're not my specialism. Equally seaweeds along the Devonshire coastline demand more attention than I can give them between these pages. Though 16 seaweeds are covered in my book; *Seaweed Foraging in Cornwall and the Isles of Scilly*, please don't be put off by the title, obviously the weeds ignore county borders and thrive in Devon too!

HOW TO USE THIS BOOK

Laid out from A-Z (Alexanders to Sorrel), each plant is covered through ID photos, distinguishing features, nutritional and medicinal benefits, suggested uses and step-by-step recipes accompanied by recipe photos, as well as a seasonal picking chart (page 9). The book is small and light and built to fit into your pocket, to be taken out and used again and again. It is also designed to complement my previous pocket books as these are also very relevant to Devon. These are as follows and contain plenty more recipes for you to enjoy:

- *Wild Food Foraging in Cornwall and the Isles of Scily* (WFF in C&IOS)
- *Seaweed Foraging in Cornwall and the Isles of Scilly* (SF in C&IOS)
- *Wild and Sweet* (W&S)

I hope this simple layout is both useful and inspiring for you.

SEASONAL CHART

Each plant has a prime growing season and some have a secondary season as well. While the berries and fruits shared in this book ripen and appear just once a year, wild foods such as leafy greens often return in autumn. Equally some berries, seeds and spices may remain on the plant for much of winter while the foliage (leaves) of many plants can be foraged in small amounts prior to their spring growth when they grow larger and more profusely.

Please take this chart as a loose guide; seasons, areas and plants can vary.

Wild Food Foraging Calendar — Devon

WILD FOOD	SPRING			SUMMER			AUTUMN			WINTER		
	MAR	APR	MAY	JUN	JUL	AUG	SEP	OCT	NOV	DEC	JAN	FEB
Alexanders (leaves)	▒	▒	▒							▒	▒	▒
Alexander Seeds (seeds)						▒	█	█	█	▒	▒	▒
Blackthorn/Sloes (fruits)							█	█	▒	▒		
Bramble/Blackberries (fruits)						▒	█	█	█			
Carrot Seeds (seeds)						▒	█	█	█	▒		
Fennel Leaves (leaves)		▒	▒	▒	▒							
Fennel Flowers (flowers)				▒	▒	▒						
Garlic (Wild) (leaves)	▒	▒	▒									
Gorse (flowers)	▒	▒	▒	▒	▒	▒	▒	▒	▒	▒	▒	▒
Hairy Bittercress (leaves)	▒	▒	▒	▒	▒	▒	▒	▒	▒	▒	▒	▒
Haw Berries/Hawthorn (fruits)							█	█	█	█	█	█
Garlic Mustard (leaves)	▒	▒	▒	▒								
Nettles (Stinging) (leaves)	▒	▒	▒				▒	▒	▒	▒		
Rowan Berries/Mountain Ash (fruits)							█	█	█	▒	▒	
Pennywort/Navelwort (leaves)	▒	▒	▒	▒			▒	▒	▒	▒	▒	▒
Rock Samphire (leaves)			▒	▒	▒	▒	▒					
Sea Radish (leaves)		▒	▒	▒	▒							
Sea Beet/Spinach (leaves)	▒	▒	▒				▒	▒	▒			
Sorrel (Common) (leaves)	▒	▒	▒	▒			▒	▒	▒			
Sorrel (Wood) (leaves)	▒	▒	▒	▒			▒	▒	▒			

KEY
Leaves · Seeds · Fruits and berries · Flowers
Darker colour: best time · Pale colour: secondary time

FORAGING GUIDELINES, SAFETY, SUSTAINABILITY AND THE LAW

Foraging done well is a wonderful way to live in harmony with nature, taking no more than we need and leaving plenty for the soil, insects, animals and birds. Done badly, it strips our earth of vital nutrients and deprives other beings of their healthy wild-life – a balance that we all need. Getting familiar with the law and these sensible guidelines can help you feel confident in your foraging tactics and reassured that you are being responsible and ethical.

Wild foods have a fantastic array of nutritional and medicinal benefits. In particular higher oil over carbohydrate content, a vast array of vitamins and minerals and trace elements. Like all foods, allergic reactions may occur in relation to any wild foods, and some foods are not compatible with certain medication or health conditions. Please check with your doctor, GP and/or medical herbalist about particular compounds or foods to avoid in these situations.

A good knowledge of plants and a humble approach to learning about them is a useful starting point. Over-confidence can lead to identification mistakes which might taste unpleasant, be sickening or fatal. The power of plants is not to be under-estimated. In particular the Umbellifer family, also known as the Carrot family (*Apiaceace*) have some deadly poisonous members. Alexanders (page 14), Wild Carrot (page 32) and Wild Fennel (page 36) are all members of this plant family. Remember to follow the golden rule: **if you're not sure, don't pick or eat it.**

British law states that we all have access to wild food for personal use (not commercial) on common land. Unfortunately, ownership and regulations are complex here in the UK and it is not always easy to find out who owns or manages a piece of land. The Wildlife and Countryside Act (1981), the Theft Act (1968) as well as guidelines for local national parks and other public areas are advisable documents to familiar yourself with. Meanwhile, here are some suggestions shown on the following page.

FORAGING GUIDELINES

- Always seek permission from the landowner, follow conservation laws, and avoid picking in protected areas such as Sites of Special Scientific Interest (SSSI).

- If unsure, don't pick the plant; check with a foraging expert (not just a generalised website). I run foraging courses and private forays for this reason.

- Only pick where there is an abundance and never more than 30% of foliage or 20% of seeds or flowers.

- Consider using scissors to help you take just the parts you want.

- It is illegal to dig up roots without permission from the landowner.

- Respect local wildlife; stick to paths and rights of way, or at least stray sensitively.

- Pick away from sources of pollution, including pesticides and pick around clean water sources.

- Rinse all foraged foods before using.

- Never pick rare plants (no plants listed in this book are rare).

- Pick for personal use only.

- Take what you need and leave the rest; vary picking sites, and leave areas as undisturbed as possible.

- Foraging starts at home – get to know (and increase) the edible weeds in your own back garden.

NOTES FOR THE COOK

Cooking with foraged ingredients may take more preparation time, so be as relaxed as possible, include helping hands, and take your time to enjoy this age-old process of preparing and cooking. Feel free to adapt and improve these recipes for your own preferences.

Local ingredients

Devon has many producers of high-quality local ingredients. Please support them at Farmers' and Country markets, farmshops, homemade stalls, delicatessens, and some local-orientated stores. Products include sea salt, fish, seafood, eggs, cheeses, butter, cream and milk, meats, honey, flour and vegetables.

CONVERSIONS

All measurements are metric. Oven temperatures are for conventional electric ovens. Here are some equivalents:

500ml	18 fl oz	8g	¼oz
600ml	21 fl oz	10g	½oz
700ml	25 fl oz	20g	¾oz
1 litre	1¾ pints	25g	1oz
2 litres	3½ pints	40g	1½oz
		60g	2oz
		120g	4oz

Oven temperatures

160°C	fan 140°C	325°F	gas 3
180°C	fan 160°C	350°F	gas 4
190°C	fan 170°C	375°F	gas 5
200°C	fan 180°C	400°F	gas 6
220°C	fan 200°C	425°F	gas 7

Length

2cm	1 inch		150g	5oz
5cm	2 inch		175g	6oz
7cm	3 inch		200g	7oz
20cm	8 inch			
75cm	30 inch		250g	9oz
1m	39 inch	3¼ ft	350g	12oz ¾lb
2m	78¾ inch	6½ ft	450g	1lb
			500g	1lb 2oz

Weight

5ml	1 tsp	600g	1lb 5oz
10ml	1 dessertspoon	680g	1½ lb
15ml	1 tbsp	700g	1lb 8oz
		1kg	2lb 3oz

Metric/imperial

75ml	3 fl oz	5 tbsp
125ml	4 fl oz	7 tbsp
150ml	¼ pint	
200ml	7 fl oz	
250ml	9 fl oz	
300ml	10½ fl oz	½ pint
350ml	12 fl oz	
400ml	14 fl oz	

ALEXANDERS/BLACK LOVAGE

Smyrnium olusatrum

Where	Mostly the southern coast, roadsides and hedgerows near the coast.
How abundant	Very, where found (considered invasive in places).
Edible parts	All – leaves, young stems, large stems peeled (before they get too fibrous), flowers, seeds, roots.
Season	Winter to early spring – leaves and young stems. Spring larger stems and flowers. Summer to winter – seeds.
Nutritional/ medicinal	Considered high in vitamins and minerals, including vitamin C and potassium. Seeds contain protein, carbohydrates and oils. Avoid if you have a celery allergy.

Get the ID right!
- Hairless plant, grows to 1.25m.
- Leaves dark green and glossy with toothed edge, stems and leaves grow in threes.
- Flowers greeny-yellow, never white, umbellifer-shaped (umbrella-like).
- Stems ribbed, maybe purple/reddish stripes.
- Seeds three-dimensional, ridged, black, sometimes with a whitish tinge.

Suggested recipes and uses
Leaves and young stems in a simple soup, or raw in a salsa verde. Young stems candied. Boil larger stems, using the liquid as stock for risottos (see WFF in C&IOS) or rice pudding. Grind chop/seeds and add to bread, chocolate truffles, curries, cheese biscuits, orange shortbreads.

Tips
Late spring use large stems for stock (too fibrous to use as a vegetable). Dried seeds can be stored for months before using. Although the roots are edible this plant is a perennial so the roots maybe years old and far too fibrous. Permission from the landowner is always needed to dig up roots.

Originally brought over by the Romans and have since naturalised along the southern coast. An aromatic leafy green, herb and a spice (seeds). Alexanders were used before the 'trend' of using celery took over.

ALEXANDERS, TOMATO AND BUTTER BEAN STEW

SERVES 4

An aromatic dish with the warming flavours of tomato and alexanders in this nourishing bean stew.

INGREDIENTS

- 1 tbsp olive oil
- 1 red onion
- 50g young alexander stems (0.5-1cm diameter)
- 1 clove of garlic
- 1 large carrot, diced
- 2 x 400g tins of chopped tomatoes
- 25-40g chopped alexander leaves
- 400g cooked butter beans (without liquid)
- salt and pepper (to taste)

Heat the olive oil over a medium heat in a medium to large saucepan and finely chop the onion, alexander stems and garlic and keep separate. When the oil is hot, add the onion and allow to sweat for a couple of minutes, add the alexander stems and stir occasionally for another 2 minutes or until the onion is translucent.

Stir in the garlic for one minute before adding the chopped tomatoes and diced carrots. Bring to a simmer, if the consistency looks too thick add 1-2 tablespoons of water and add the alexander leaves.

Place the lid on the saucepan and leave to cook for 10 minutes.

Add the butter beans and simmer for another 10 minutes, taste and add salt and pepper if needed. Serve hot with squares of Alexander Seeded Focaccia (page 19).

ALEXANDER SEEDED FOCACCIA BREAD

MAKES 1 LOAF

Alexander seeds add a wonderful bitter spice to this moreish loaf, the seeds combining beautifully with the flavours of sea salt and olive oil.

INGREDIENTS

- 1 tbsp + 1 tsp black alexander seeds*
- 500g strong white bread flour
- 1 tsp quick yeast
- a pinch of sugar
- 1 tsp sea salt
- 5 tbsp olive oil
- 350ml warm water

Firstly roughly chop the alexander seeds*, just enough to break them and release their flavour. Put 1 teaspoon of them aside. Place the flour in a large bowl with the yeast, sugar, 1 tablespoon of chopped seeds, half the salt and 2 tablespoons of the olive oil. Gradually add the warm water and mix together until there's enough liquid to form a soft dough and knead for 5-10 minutes. Cover the bowl and leave in a warm place for an hour or overnight until it doubles in size.

Grease a 30 × 30cm tin or similar sized baking tin. Stretch the dough into the greased tin and leave to rise for an hour or until doubled in size again. Use your finger to create dimples across the top. Grind the remaining teaspoon of alexander seeds with the remaining salt and sprinkle evenly across the dough, followed by another 2 tablespoons of olive oil.

Preheat the oven to 220°C/fan 200°C/425°F/ gas mark 7. Bake for 20 minutes until golden on top and the bread is coming away from the sides. Pour over the last tablespoon of oil and set aside for 10 minutes before removing onto a cooling rack. Enjoy with bean stew, or pesto and cheeses.

*If early in the season it might be easy to chop them on a chopping board or in a pestle and mortar. If later in the season it may be easier to soak them in cold water for 10 minutes, making them easier to break.

BLACKTHORN/SLOE
Prunus spinosa

Where	Woods, scrubland, hedgerows, right up to sea cliffs.
How abundant	Very where found, create dense thickets.
Edible parts	Fruits (after first frost), flowers in moderation as contain cyanide.
Season	Late summer, autumn.
Nutritional/ medicinal	Contains tannins, organic acids, sugars, vitamin C. Duiretic and considered supportive for kidneys, bladder and stomach.

Small, dark and round fruits, a member of the plum family. Blackthorn refers to the dark bark and the long thorns which are more visible once the leaves have fallen.

Get the ID right!

- Stiff, thorny shrub, grows up to 4m; white flowers appear before the leaves in early spring.
- Leaves matt and oval, coming into a pointed tip, with a slightly toothed edge.
- Purplish fruits, like very small plums (1-2cm diameter) with a large stone inside.

Suggested recipes and uses
Jam (page 22) and sauces to accompany red meats or game or to use in gravies. Add with other wild fruits to fruit vinegar. An essential in sloe gin, destone and use alcohol-soaked fruits for fruit compote, in trifle, or in chocolate (WFF C&IOS, page 27). More sweet, sloe recipes can be found in W&S.

Tips
The spikes of blackthorn are very sharp with the reputation of creating wounds that may go septic. Pick carefully or with thick gloves. Freezing the fruits (to mimic the first frost) helps soften the skins and sweeten them. Picking and freezing them before the first frost ensures you get some before they shrivel on the shrub.

SLOE AND APPLE JAM

MAKES 1.2KG

A tart, thick and plummy jam. Use to sandwich sponge cakes together or in Sloe and Apple Crumble Slices (page 25), also gorgeous with cheese.

INGREDIENTS

- 500g sloes (washed, stalks removed)
- 300ml water
- 500g cooking apples, washed
- 750g soft brown sugar

Add the sloes and water to a medium-large saucepan. Bring to the boil, cover and simmer for 10 minutes or until soft.

Using the back of a wooden spoon, press the fruits and liquid through a colander into a large bowl. The more pulp you press through the better, there should be about 500ml.

Chop the apples and discard the cores. Add to the saucepan along with the sloe pulp. Bring to the boil and simmer until the apple has broken down (5-10 minutes).

Lower the heat and add the sugar, stirring until dissolved. Bring to a medium to high heat and allow to bubble until it reaches jam setting point (105°C/221°F).

Keep the lid half covering the pan to protect yourself from hot, spitting, sugary liquid. Pour into clean, sterilised jars.

SLOE AND APPLE CRUMBLE SLICES

MAKES 9 SLICES

A sweet, oatmeal slice with a fruity sloe and apple jam centre and crumble topping.

INGREDIENTS

- 170g butter, melted
- 100g wholemeal flour
- 50g plain flour
- 110g porridge oats, raw
- ¼ tsp baking powder
- 50g soft brown sugar
- 175g sloe and apple jam

Grease a 20cm x 20cm baking tin and preheat the oven to 180°C/fan 160°C/ 350°F/gas mark 4. Melt the butter in a small saucepan over a low heat. Put aside to cool. In a large bowl, combine the flours, porridge oats, baking powder and sugar.

Stir in the melted butter until the dough is firm and consistent. Press three-quarters of the mixture into the tin to make an even base.

Gently spread the jam across the pressed dough until the whole surface is covered. Crumble the rest of the dough across the top and bake for 25-30 minutes or until golden. Allow to cool before slicing.

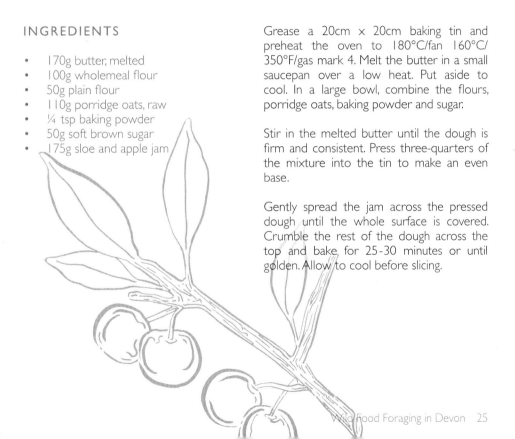

BRAMBLE/BLACKBERRY
Rubus fruticosus

Where	Hedgerows, wasteland, moorland, any spare patch of ground.
How abundant	Very.
Edible parts	Fruits when black and come away easily. Leaf buds raw, larger stems and leaves for tea.
Season	Late summer and autumn. Leaves in spring.
Nutritional/ medicinal	Rich in vitamin C, fibre, and contains sugars and pectin. Seeds contain omega 3 and 6. Leaves have antiseptic, anti-fungal properties and are good for upset stomachs, colds and flu.

The most commonly foraged wild fruit in Britain and arguably our most common fruit due to the bramble's ability to grow extremely fast and re-route whenever a stem touches the ground.

Get the ID right!
- Thick, spiny stems that spread up to 3m and root when they touch the ground.
- Toothed, oval leaves that come into a point, with prickles on back of leaf spines.
- White or pink flowers.
- Red, bulbous fruits that blacken when ripe.

Suggested recipes and uses
For jam, use fruit alone (WFF in C&IOS, page 31) or with apple. Jelly and syrups can be made from leaves, stems or fruits (strain through a jelly bag). Use leftover seeds and fibre in bread, crackers or granola. Excellent in fruit vinegars; use fruits or leaves in herbal tea infusions and salads, or fruits in sweet baking.

Tips
There are officially over 400 varieties of brambles, all with a slightly different taste, shape and size. If you find a tasty patch it might be a good variety, not just the weather and soil.

BLACKBERRY CORDIAL

MAKES 275 ML

A richly flavoured cordial to dilute for drinks or drizzle over cakes and desserts. Remember to keep the leftover pulp for making Blackberry Seeded Granola (page 31).

INGREDIENTS

- 400g blackberries
- 1 tbsp water
- 110g soft brown sugar

Place the fruits and water in a medium saucepan over a medium heat. Using the back of a wooden spoon, squash the fruits to help release the juice.

Cover and simmer for 10 minutes. Strain through a jelly bag, muslin or nylon cloth and leave to drip through for at least 30 minutes.

Return the liquid to a clean pan along with the sugar and stir over a medium, simmering heat for 5 minutes then store in a sterilised bottle.

BLACKBERRY SEEDED GRANOLA

Fruity, chewy and crunchy, this simple granola is made by using the discarded blackberry seeds and fibre from blackberry cordial. Surprisingly flavourful, it's the perfect topping for hot porridge, with a little blackberry cordial, or enjoy on its own as a breakfast cereal.

INGREDIENTS

- 115ml (190g) honey
- 110ml (110g) vegetable oil
- 150g blackberry pulp (left from making the cordial)
- 350g jumbo oats

Combine the honey and oil in a small saucepan and heat over a low heat until melted and combined. Put aside.

Heat the oven to 170°C/fan 150°C/338°F/ gas mark 4.5 and line a large baking tray with baking paper. When the honey/oil blend is cooled to room temperature, pour into a large bowl and add the blackberry pulp and the oats. Stir well to combine then spoon onto the baking tray and spread out evenly. Press the mixture down a little and bake for 15 minutes. Take out of the oven and stir, then return for a further 15 minutes before stirring again.

The mixture will take a little longer than normal granola to bake as the blackberry pulp is moist, so keep checking and turning the mixture every five to 10 minutes or until brown and slightly crisp throughout.

If you like granola with chunky clusters, press the mixture down between mixing it. Take out of the oven and leave to cool, it will harden more as it cools.

Store in a large jar and enjoy liberally, use within 1 month.

CARROT (WILD)
Daucus carota

Where	Coastal areas from cliffs down to the beach.
How abundant	Very in specific areas.
Edible parts	Seeds (avoid if pregnant), roots (permission needed from landowner to dig up. They're small and fibrous).
Season	Late summer to autumn (seeds).
Nutritional/ medicinal	Good for digestive ailments, contains vitamin B complex, sugars, pectin. Seeds can be abortive and should not be digested if pregnant or trying to get pregnant

A stunning coastal flower and the unassuming origin of the sweet, orange root vegetables we know as carrots. The seeds are complex in flavour and surprisingly aromatic.

Get the ID right!
- Grows up to 75cm tall (though often smaller), with a stout, rough, hairy stem.
- Flowers are umbelliferous (umbrella-like), with long, small leaves coming down direct from the base of the flower head.
- Flowers can be white, white with a single pink/red flower in the middle, mottled white and pink, or completely pink.
- Leaves are feathery, similar to cultivated carrot.

Suggested recipes and uses
Seeds to flavour cakes, cookies (page 34) and bread (WFF in C&IOS, page 79) or toasted along with other seeds and spices and sprinkled onto dhal, soup or salads.

Tips
The roots are very fibrous, so seeds are preferable. Gather the seeds by scooping out a few seeds from each seed-head and leaving the majority behind and intact on the plant (bottom left photo). Use the seeds whole for the best flavour, although grinding them temporarily releases a lovely aroma this disappears quickly.

HONEY AND CARROT SEED COOKIES

MAKES 12

A wholesome, rustic cookie with a comforting flavour or honey, butter and fragrant carrot seeds.

INGREDIENTS

- 120g local honey
- 25g butter
- 200g spelt or wholemeal flour
- 2 tsp baking powder
- 4 tsp dried carrot seeds

Preheat the oven to 175°C/fan 155°C/347°F/ gas mark 3.5. Heat the honey and butter slowly in a saucepan until melted, then take off the heat.

Mix all the dry ingredients together in a bowl, then add slowly to the honey and butter, mixing thoroughly. The mixture should be sticky and stiff.

Grease a baking tray. Shape the mixture into balls (you may need a little extra flour for this) and place on the baking tray about 5cm apart.

Flatten them into cookie-like shapes, and bake for 20-25 minutes, or until golden. Enjoy on their own or with hot tea.

FENNEL (WILD)
Foeniculum vulgare

Where	Coastal areas and gardens.
How abundant	Varies, common in places, also grows well in gardens.
Edible parts	Leaves, flowers, seeds.
Season	Leaves in spring/early summer, flowers in summer, seeds late summer/autumn.
Nutritional/ medicinal	A traditional digestive that helps break down fatty foods, reduces bloating and can even help menstrual pains. Has been proved to increase milk flow in breastfeeding mothers.

A refreshing aniseed flavour from these leggy and pretty coastal plants that are renowned for their excellent medicinal qualities.

Get the ID right!
- Grows up to 1.2m high, hairless stems which are hollow when old.
- Feathery leaves similar to dill, pale grey-green in colour.
- Flowers are yellow, umbelliferous (umbrella-like), and scent is of fresh aniseed.
- Seeds are grey-green to brown, depending on how fresh.

Suggested recipes and uses
Chop and mix leaves with butter for a herb butter (page 102). Add to salads, bake with fish, use in risotto, omelettes or similar. Make tempura with the flower heads, grind seeds into bread, sweet biscuits, or savoury dishes. Also good as a tea, or in desserts such as sorbet.

Tips
The roots of wild fennel are different from the cultivated kind. With the wild one, use only the aerial parts.

FENNEL FLOWER FRITTERS

SERVES 4

These flower fritters can be made sweet or savoury. Serve alongside fish with a lemon dressing or paired with the soft, refreshing Fennel Leaf Sorbet (page 41).

INGREDIENTS

- 200ml cold milk
- 1 large egg, beaten
- 90g sifted plain flour
- sunflower oil for frying
- 12 fennel flower heads (stalk intact to hold onto when frying)
- icing sugar to decorate (optional)

Pour the milk into a mixing bowl, mix in the beaten egg, add the flour and roughly fold in with a fork. Do not beat, as the batter should be lumpy.

Heat the oil in a wok or a frying pan with 1-2cm depth of oil. When hot, hold flower heads by the stalk, wipe them through the batter to cover, and fry gently in the oil until golden brown.

Remove from the oil and drain on a paper towel. To serve, snip the main stalk off each flower, and enjoy warm or cold.

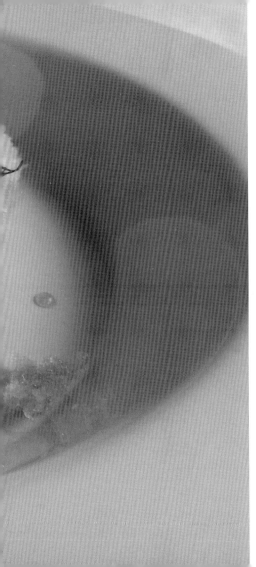

FENNEL LEAF SORBET

SERVES 4

A sweet, melt-in-the-mouth treat infused with the uplifting flavour of wild fennel.

INGREDIENTS

- 30g fennel foliage
  (leaves and small stalks)
- 240ml water
- 80g sugar

Wash and chop the fennel, place in a large heat-proof bowl and pour on 150ml of boiling water. Cover and leave overnight.

Meanwhile, in a small saucepan add the sugar to 90ml of water, stir and bring to the boil before leaving to cool. When the infused fennel is ready, blend it in a food blender before straining it through a fine sieve, squeezing until all the liquid is removed.

Mix the sugar syrup with the infused liquid and churn in an ice-cream maker or place in ice-lolly moulds. Alternatively, transfer to a metal baking tin and place in the freezer, stirring with a fork every half an hour until frozen, smooth and creamy.

Keep in the freezer until required.

GARLIC (WILD), RAMSONS
Allium ursinum

Where	Moist woodlands, shady areas.
How abundant	Very, in the right habitats.
Edible parts	Leaves, stems, flowers, roots (permission is needed to dig up the roots).
Season	Spring.
Nutritional/ medicinal	Contains high amounts of magnesium, is good for cardiovascular and respiratory health and digestive health.

Carpets of wild garlic are hard to ignore. Their scent and abundance captures the heart of many foragers, including my own. Devon farmers have been known to have their cow's milk rejected for the garlicky smell, if the herd have eaten wild garlic.

Get the ID right!
- Triangular stem, grows to 45cm.
- Broad leaves, slightly ridged.
- Flowers are star-like in an umbrella structure with up to 20 flowers on every flower-head.
- Seeds are small, green and bulbous and follow after the flowers.

Suggested recipes and uses
Can be used as a fresh herb in many dishes from rice to sauces to stews as well as raw in salads and as garnishes. Use to flavour butter (page 102).

Tips
Some get a stomach upset from eating it or consuming large amounts of it, allergic reactions have been known. Over picking the seed pods can detrimentally effect the following year's growth.

WILD GARLIC PESTO

MAKES 260G (APPROX)

A stunning and simple pesto that always goes down a treat. Mix into pasta, rice, any grain or potatoes, spread onto toast or use as a component in a Savoury Wild Garlic Cream Tea (page 51).

INGREDIENTS

- 120-150ml virgin olive oil
- juice of half a lemon
- 50g walnuts or hazelnuts
- 150g wild garlic leaves and stems
- 60g parmesan cheese, grated
- salt and pepper (to taste)

Blend together the oil, lemon juice and nuts and blitz until smooth or until the nuts are a texture you're happy with for the pesto.

Add the garlic and cheese and blitz again. Taste and season with salt and pepper according to your preference.

Alternatively, you can create this by hand by crushing the nuts in a pestle and mortar or similar, finely chopping the garlic and combining everything together.

Keeps for up to a week in the fridge.

WILD GARLIC FLOWER CREAM

A garlic flavoured cream that can be made using cream cheese, mascarpone cheese or clotted cream! Use on savoury dishes such as hot pasta or as part of a Savoury Wild Garlic Cream Tea (page 51).

INGREDIENTS

- 20 wild garlic flower heads and stalks
- 200g cream cheese, mascarpone cheese or clotted cream

Chop the garlic flower heads and finely chop the stalks.

Stir into the cheese or cream of your choice.

Keeps in a sealed container for up to 5 days in the fridge.

WILD GARLIC SCONES

MAKES 13-14

Savoury scones with the rich flavours of garlic and cheese in a perfectly light dough. These are great smothered with sorrel butter (page 102) or enjoy as part of a Savoury Wild Garlic Cream Tea (page 51)!

INGREDIENTS

- 250g plain flour
- 50g wholemeal flour
- 5 level tsp baking powder
- large pinch sea salt
- 75g butter, cold
- 30g wild garlic leaves
- 140g cheddar cheese, grated
- 120 - 130ml milk (I use full-fat)

Grease a large baking tray. Preheat the oven to 200°C/fan 180°C/400°F/gas mark 6.

Add the flours, baking powder and salt to a large bowl, combine well. Cube the butter, add to the flour and combine in a food processor or rub by hand to create breadcrumbs.

Finely chop the garlic leaves and add in, along with 120g of the cheese. Gradually stir in the milk, adding just enough to bring the dough together, don't over stir.

There may be some milk leftover, which is fine. Lightly dust a clean surface with flour and roll out the dough to about 2cm (1 inch) thick). Use a 7cm (3 inch) biscuit cutter and cut as many scones as possible.

You may need to reroll the dough to cut the last couple of shapes. Place on the baking tray with some space between each. Lightly brush the tops with milk and sprinkle on the remaining cheese.

Bake for 15 mins.

Transfer to a cooling rack and serve warm or keep for up to 5 days in an airtight container.

SAVOURY WILD GARLIC CREAM TEA

MAKES 13-14

The tradition in Devon is 'cream first' followed by jam. Here I've recreated this with a savoury theme – cream first followed by pesto. Use recipes on pages 44-48 and assemble according to your taste to create this delicious Savoury Wild Garlic Cream Tea.

GARLIC MUSTARD, JACK BY THE HEDGE
Alliaria petiolata

Where	Roadsides, hedges, partially shady areas.
How abundant	Common where found.
Edible parts	Leaves, flowers.
Season	Spring to early summer.
Nutritional/ medicinal	Contains vitamins A, C, E, some B vitamins and omega 3 as well as copper, iron, potassium, magnesium, selenium and manganese. Has been used very little as a medicine.

A member of the brassica (cabbage) family. A common hedgerow green with a distinct mustard-smell and a hint of garlic when the leaves are crushed.

Get the ID right!
- Grows up to 1m high, biennial (2yr life span).
- Heart-shaped leaves with toothed edges and pale green in colour.
- White flowers with 4 petals which make a cross-shape, as is common in this crucifer family.
- Seed-heads up to 7cm long.

Suggested recipes and uses
Add to salad and use as a garnish for savoury dishes. Finely chop and add to pesto or salsa verde. Chop and blend with butter (page 102), serve with fish or simply fry until crispy.

Tips
Pick on minor roads or away from roads completely. Blanching the leaves reduces the intensity of their taste but still gives a good, mustardy flavour.

HEDGE MUSTARD DOLMADES

SERVES 4 | 8-10 AS A STARTER | MAKES 40

The pungent flavour of these wild leaves and their potential size lend them perfectly for this Greek delicacy. This is a simplified version, replacing the traditional vine leaves.

INGREDIENTS

- 40 large hedge mustard leaves (10/12cm across if possible)
- 200g risotto rice
- 700ml hot vegetable stock
- 1 bay leaf (optional)
- 1 medium onion
- 1 ½ tbsp olive oil
- 1 tsp cinnamon
- 1 tsp ground coriander
- 1 tbsp tomato paste
- 125g local minced beef (or replace with veggies)
- 3 tbsp finely chopped hedge mustard leaves

For the Dressing (optional)
- 6 tbsp finely chopped hedge mustard leaves
- 2 tbsp preserved lemons
- 4 tbsp olive oil

First blanch the large leaves for 15 seconds in boiling water. Have a large bowl of ice-cold water nearby and use a slotted spoon or similar to take the leaves out of the hot and into the cold water to stop them cooking further. Leave for a few minutes to cool. Carefully squeeze out the excess water and very carefully, unfold the leaves and flatten onto a plate or board.

Bring the rice to the boil in a small saucepan along with the hot stock and bay leaf (if using), cover and simmer for 15-20 minutes or until cooked and put aside. Finely chop the onion. Heat the oil in a frying pan and when hot, add the onion, stirring until translucent. Add the spices, tomato paste and mince and stir to combine until the meat browns. Toss in the chopped hedge mustard leaves and cook for a further 5 minutes. Take off the heat and mix in the rice thoroughly and put aside.

To assemble the dolmades, take a dessertspoon of mixture and place in the centre of a single leaf. The amount of mixture will vary depending on the size of the leaf. Don't overload. Shape the mixture

into a loose sausage shape and start to roll (wide end first), fold in the sides and complete the roll before placing on a flat surface. Continue with all the leaves and mixture. These can be eaten warm or cold and are delicious undressed. For an added layer of Greek flavours, blend together the rest of the leaves, preserved lemon and olive oil and drizzle over the dolmades before serving.

GORSE
Ulex europaeus or Ulex gallii

Where	Moors, heathland right up to the coast.
How abundant	Very, where found.
Edible parts	Flowers.
Season	All year around, most abundant in spring, then again in autumn and winter (depending on variety).
Nutritional/ medicinal	Thought to counter hopelessness and despair in homeopathy and flower remedies.

The bright yellow of gorse flowers is an uplifting sight in winter, or a hazy moorland view at other times.

Get the ID right!
- Evergreen shrub, grows to 1.5-2m high.
- Spiky foliage, bright yellow flowers with a coconut scent (in full sun).
- Furry seed pods that you can hear pop open in late summer.
- Common gorse (Ulex europaeus) flowers in spring/early summer. It is larger than Western gorse (Ulex gallii), and the latter, or a hybrid of the two, flowers the rest of the year.

Suggested recipes and uses
Infusions for tea, flower syrups, sorbet, ice-cream, custard or macaroons, or use in rice pudding. Decorate salads or creamy coconut curries. Make wine from the flowers, or pickle the buds and add to salads. More recipes in W&S.

Tips
The spikes are sharp, so pick flowers with gloves on, and in full sun to capture their scent. Dried flowers (page 59) have a more concentrated scent for flavouring foods. This plant can smell strongly of coconut, but the scent in cooking and eating is fainter and more floral.

GORSE FLOWER RICE PUDDING WITH GORSE FLOWER SYRUP

SERVES 4

A traditionally made rice pudding with a delicate and wild texture. Particularly good drizzled with gorse flower syrup.

FOR THE PUDDING:

INGREDIENTS

- 50g fresh gorse flowers
- 1.3 litres full-fat milk
- 100g pudding or risotto rice
- 50g golden granulated sugar
- 25g butter
- 4-8 tbsp gorse flower syrup

Preheat the oven to 180°C/160°C fan/ 350°F/gas mark 4. Simmer the fresh gorse flowers in milk for 15 minutes, then blend with a food blender to help break up the flower pods.

Meanwhile, put the rice, sugar and butter in an ovenproof dish and pour on the infused milk. Bake in the oven for 1 ½ hours, or until all the milk is absorbed and the rice is soft and cooked.

There will be a cooked, milky skin over the dish. Serve the rice pudding hot with generous spoonfuls of syrup over each portion.

―――――――――

FOR THE SYRUP:

INGREDIENTS

- 16g dried gorse flowers (2 handfuls) or 20-25g semi-dried flowers*
- 75g golden granulated sugar
- water, to cover the flowers and sugar

Place the dried or semi-dried gorse flowers and sugar in a small pan and cover with just enough hot water.

Simmer for 10 minutes before straining through a fine sieve or muslin cloth, making sure you get every last drop.

Store in a sterilised bottle or drizzle immediately over portions of Gorse Flower Rice Pudding.

*To dry flowers for the syrup: spread out freshly picked flowers in the sun or a warm place for 48 hours, or dry in the oven at the lowest temperature for 2-4 hours. Semi-dried flowers are also fine.

HAIRY BITTERCRESS
Cardamine hirsuta

Where	Riversides, muddy puddles, damp and moist areas, flower beds.
How abundant	An abundant weed where found.
Edible parts	All parts are edible.
Season	Mostly spring, found throughout the year.
Nutritional/ medicinal	Contains vitamin C, beta-carotene and glucosinolates. The brassica family have been linked to stimulating the immune system and reducing the risk of cancers.

A small member of the brassica (cabbage) family with a spicy, peppery flavour.

Get the ID right!
- Grows to 30cm tall but often as small as 5-15cm tall.
- Small white flowers each with four petals to make a cross.
- Leaf shape reminiscent of the leaves of watercress but on a smaller scale – hairy leaves, round-ish with a wavy edge.
- Long, narrow, fibrous seed pods.

Suggested recipes and uses
Use as a salad or raw as a garnish. Dress with mayonnaise (page 62) or salad dressing if you wish.

Tips
Chop and use immediately and as fresh as possible. Don't complicate with adding other strong flavours. Choose picking areas carefully as it is best eaten raw, so you should be certain of good water quality. I don't suggest picking from muddy, waterlogged footpaths!

HAIRY BITTERCRESS AND EGG MAYO

SERVES 2

An easy snack with a wild twist. The bittercress gives a lovely crunch and a bit of fiery burst to this classic filling. It's perfect on toast or as a sandwich filler.

INGREDIENTS

- 2 free-range eggs
- 25g hairy bittercress
- 2 tbsp mayonnaise
- salt and pepper (optional)

Place the eggs in a small saucepan and cover with cold water. Bring to the boil and simmer for 10 minutes for the classic hard-boiled centre.

Take out of the water with a spoon and leave to cool before peeling off the shell. If you can't wait for the eggs to cool, place in a bowl of cold water to help the process along.

Wash thoroughly and roughly chop the bittercress and add to a medium bowl with the mayonnaise and de-shelled eggs.

Mash together with a fork and serve. Remember to taste and add a little salt and pepper, if using. Best eaten immediately.

HAW BERRIES, HAWTHORN TREE, MAY TREE

Crataegus monogyna

Where	Deciduous woodlands, field boundaries and hilltops.
How abundant	Common tree where found.
Edible parts	Berries (not the stones), young leaves, flowers.
Season	Autumn, and potentially through winter, young leaves (spring), flowers (late spring/early summer).
Nutritional/ medicinal	Known to improve and regulate heart health. Full of vitamins including; C, B1, B2, B3 and B12. Seek professional medical advice before eating if on heart medication.

Also known as the bread and cheese tree (as so many parts are edible), or the May tree as this is the month when the flowers appear (top right photo). The tree is a characteristic vision on a hillside – shaped by the wind.

Get the ID right!
- Can grow up to 4m tall.
- Branches are thorny and often gnarled in shape.
- Berries are 1cm across growing in clusters. Each is shaped like a mini-apple and red in colour, going deeper in colour towards winter. Each berry harbours a sizeable stone in its centre.
- Leaves are crown-shaped, or emblem-shaped with 3 lobes at the top and 2 lower lobes pointing outwards.

Suggested recipes and uses
Berries taste a little like a dry apple/apple peel, so not hugely appealing, but definitely worth trying. Cook berries for jam or fruit leather (W&S book), relish or chutney and serve with bread and cheese.

Tips
Berries need to be flavoured if cooked. The flowers are fertilised by flies, so best used for hot tea infusions and not raw. Berries turn brown when frozen and/or cooked – this is natural.

HAW BERRY CHUTNEY

MAKES 400G (APPROX.)

A hearty, versatile chutney with a spicy kick. Use instead of brown sauce or barbeque sauce with barbequed meats, or as a chutney alongside cheese, bread or crackers.

INGREDIENTS

- 400g haw berries (no stalks)
- 400ml water
- 100ml cider vinegar
- 1 onion, chopped
- 1 clove garlic, chopped
- ½ - 1 red chilli, chopped
- 2 tbsp balsamic vinegar
- 3 tbsp brown sugar
- 2 tsp freshly grated turmeric (½ tsp dried turmeric)
- salt and pepper (to taste)
- 1 tbsp cornflour (optional)

Rinse the berries and place in a medium saucepan with the water and cider vinegar. Bring to the boil and simmer with the lid on for 15 minutes, until the berries are tender. Place a wide-holed sieve or small-holed colander over a large, heatproof bowl and pour in the contents.

Next, using the back of a wooden spoon, press the pulp through the sieve. You'll need to put a fair amount of effort into this and it can take up to 20 minutes, there should be about 150g of pulp. Continue until you have mostly stones left in the sieve and a liquid-pulp below.

Discard the stones and place the pulp back in the saucepan along with the chopped onion, garlic and chilli, sugar and turmeric.

Bring to the boil and simmer for 5 minutes or until the onion is soft. Taste and add salt and pepper if needed. Check the consistency and if watery, sieve or sprinkle in 1 tablespoon of cornflour and cook for a couple of minutes.

Pour into a sterilised jar or two. The jar should have a rubber-sealed lid to protect it from the vinegar.

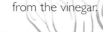

COMMON NETTLE (STINGING)
Urtica dioica

Where	Fields, hedgerows, woodlands, wasteland, gardens.
How abundant	Very.
Edible parts	Top 4 - 6 leaves (before the flowers appear), seeds of female plants.
Season	Leaves primarily in spring then autumn/winter, seeds in summer.
Nutritional/ medicinal	Contains vitamins A, B, C and iron. High in protein and calcium and a good overall nutritious boost and tonic. Helps lower blood sugar, stimulates circulation and can help relieve arthritis.

One of the best and most nutritious wild greens we have. Cooking nettles removes the sting completely.

Get the ID right!
- Grows up to 1m tall.
- Oval, hairy, dark green leaves, deeply toothed and with a pointed tip.
- The hairs (present all over the plant) sting, creating heat, itching and a throbbing pain for hours.
- Flowers greenish, sometimes tinged purple, are like catkins, attached below the leaves and coming off the main stem.

Suggested recipes and uses
Replace cooked spinach with nettles in any recipe, for example, in pasta, gnocchi, or risotto. Great in nettle & potato curry and pesto (WFF C&IOS, page 95). Nettle syrup and nettle and honey cake (W&S) are also good. Combines well with lemon or ginger. Nothing beats nettle soup though (page 70).

Tips
Pick using thick gloves. Do not pick/ eat leaves when in flower (bottom right photo). Cooking for a couple of minutes will completely remove the sting.

NETTLE SOUP

SERVES 4

A wild and delicious classic dish and a brilliant wild food to eat in spring.

INGREDIENTS

- 1 tbsp oil of frying
- 1 onion, peeled and sliced
- 2 celery stems or young, tender alexander stems (page 14), chopped (optional)
- 2 medium potatoes, peeled and chopped
- 500ml milk
- 500ml vegetable stock, hot
- 250g nettle tops, washed
- Crème Fraîche for garnish (optional)

Heat the oil in a large pan, and when hot add the onion, lower the heat and allow to sweat with the lid on for 5 minutes.

Add the celery or alexander stem, if using, and sweat for a further 5 minutes.

Next, add the potatoes, milk and stock and bring to the boil, simmering for 10 minutes or until the potatoes are soft. Carefully add the nettle tops, either with gloves or two wooden spoons and cook for a further 10 minutes.

Blend in a food processor before pouring into bowls and garnishing each with a swirl of Crème Fraîche, if using.

Enjoy immediately.

NETTLE AND POTATO FRITTERS
(WITH SORREL DIP)

MAKES 20

Simple but delicious fritters with the earthy flavour of nettles and a zing of wild garlic. Lovely served warm with sorrel dip (page 103) as a starter, snack or main course.

INGREDIENTS

- 1kg potatoes
- 150g stinging nettle tops
- a few wild garlic leaves
- ½ tsp red chilli or paprika (optional)
- salt and pepper (to taste)
- 1 free-range egg, beaten
- 3 tbsp plain flour
- oil for frying

Wash the potatoes and peel off any rough or blemished bits. I like to keep a bit of the skin to add texture, but you could peel completely if you prefer.

Chop into large chunks and bring to the boil in a large saucepan of salted water. Simmer until tender, then strain and put aside. Steam the nettle tops for 5 minutes then put aside to cool.

Mash the potato and add the spices (if using) and salt and pepper to taste. Finely chop the cooked nettle tops and wild garlic leaves. Stir into the potato, along with the beaten egg and mix in thoroughly.

Scatter the flour over a clean surface or plate. Using your hands, break off pieces of the mixture, roll into balls then flatten into patties about 6cm wide and 1cm deep and lightly flour. Continue with all the mixture. Firm up in the fridge for an hour if you have time.

Heat a little oil in a large frying pan over a medium heat. When hot, add about 4 patties at a time, making sure you have enough space around them to check and turn them over.

Cook for about 1-2 minutes on either side, or until browned. Serve warm or eat cold as a snack.

PENNYWORT/NAVELWORT
Umbilicus rupestris

Where	Stone-walls, rocks and the base of trees.
How abundant	Very.
Edible parts	Leaves and stems.
Season	Best in spring, second-best through autumn and winter.
Nutritional/ medicinal	'Wort' means plant of worth. Has been used as a poultice to treat anything from piles, mild burns, scalds, chilblains to sore breasts. Considered a diuretic and used internally for inflamed liver or spleen.

A succulent thirst-quencher of the hedgerow with a lovely firm texture and mild taste of peas.

Get the ID right!
- Grows up to 50cm tall (when in flower).
- Leaves 1- 4cm diameter (like old penny).
- Green, fleshy leaves, paler stem. Leaves dented in the middle like an inward belly button, or 'navel' and slightly scalloped edge.
- Flower is pale green or pinkish-white and bell-shaped.

Suggested recipes and uses
Best used whole in salads and garnishes or remove the stem and use as a canape base, or blended into drinks (mix with sugar syrup) or dips.

Tips
Use fresh, as these delicate plants are easily bruised and don't keep well once picked. Store in a vase or glass, with the stalks in water or in a container in the fridge. The mild flavour varies from bitter to sweet, so try in different seasons and from different growing places. When picking, snap the stem rather than pull the plant as the roots can easily become dislodged.

PENNYWORT AND CREAM CHEESE CANAPÉS

SERVES 4

This recipe can almost be done with your eyes closed. Though with eyes open, the visual effect brings a smile to any dinner table.

INGREDIENTS

- 16 large pennywort leaves (stalks snapped off and eaten or left in the hedgerow)
- 15g herbs (e.g. parsley, dill, chervil, sorrel, wild garlic)
- 150g creamy cheese (e.g. goats cheese, not too crumbly, not too gooey)

Wash the pennyworts and gently pat dry with a cloth, or wipe or dust off any dirt or debris.

Finely chop the herbs and mix with the cream cheese. I like to keep each herb separate, and use three, for variety.

Using your fingers and a teaspoon, carefully place a ball of the cream cheese mix in the middle of each leaf.

Serve as canapé or as a salad garnish.

ROCK SAMPHIRE
Crithmum maritimum

Where	Cliffs and rocks occasionally in the sand, always above the high tide mark.
How abundant	Very, in places.
Edible parts	Leaves and young stems, seeds (summer).
Season	Late spring to early summer, in autumn.
Nutritional/ medicinal	Rich in vitamin C and omega 3. Used as a digestive aid and as an anti-aging aid.

In my opinion, rock samphire is the superior, both nutritionally and in taste, of the two samphires (the other is marsh samphire, which grows in salty estuaries). A wonderful lemony and aromatic flavour.

Get the ID right!
- Grows up to 40cm in height, grey-green plant, hairless and slightly ribbed.
- Fleshy, tubular stems and flattened leaves.
- Yellow-tinged flowers, umbelliferous (umbrella-like), with bulbous seeds that come later.
- Strong citrus/aromatic scent when crushed.

Suggested recipes and uses
Cook for just 2 - 3 minutes, add to salads, use as a side vegetable with fish or seafood (WFF in C&IOS, page 70). Good in risotto, stir-fry, or serve with eggs, in feta cheese salad, or pickled with wedges of lemon and fennel seeds.

Tips
In summer the flavour of the leaves can be too strong to use successfully.

ROCK SAMPHIRE SALSA VERDE

SERVES 4 (AS A SIDE DISH)

A quick and impressive dish to whip up and serve with fish or alongside any dish that could benefit from a flavourful, green side. I like to take this to barbeques.

INGREDIENTS

- 85g rock samphire
- 3-4 spring onions
- 1 dessertspoon capers
- 1 tsp vinegar
- 1-2 tbsp olive oil
- 1 tbsp lemon (optional)
- salt and pepper (to taste)
- 2 anchovies (optional)

Wash the samphire and cook in a small amount of water for 2-3 minutes in a lidded saucepan.

The water doesn't need to cover the samphire, as it will reduce and cook in its own steam.

Remove from the pan and allow to cool. Meanwhile finely slice the spring onions and chop the capers.

When the samphire is cool enough to handle, finely chop it and mix in a bowl along with the onions, capers, vinegar, oil, salt and pepper.

Add the lemon and finely chop the anchovies, if using, and mix in thoroughly.

Keeps well in the fridge for a few days.

ROWAN BERRIES (MOUNTAIN ASH)
Sorbus aucuparia

Where	Hillsides, native woods, high altitude areas.
How abundant	Scattered.
Edible parts	Berries (after first frost or freezing and cooking).
Season	Autumn and some remain in winter.
Nutritional/ medicinal	Full of vitamin C, sorbic acid (once cooked), fibre and antioxidants.

A wonderful wild fruit with a complex, bitter flavour. Must be cooked to make it safe and palatable to eat. A favourite winter food for birds so leave plenty for them.

Get the ID right!
- Grows as a tree or shrub up to 20 metres tall.
- Clusters of orangey-red berries.
- Long, toothed leaves growing in pairs opposite each other with one at the tip.

Suggested recipes and uses
Make into syrup or cook with apple to make a jam. Can also be preserved in syrup (more recipes in W&S).

Tips
Only use after cooking as this turns the indigestible parasorbic acid into digestible sorbic acid. Also best to pick after the first frost or place in freezer (to fake the first frost), do not eat raw.

ROWAN BERRY CORDIAL

MAKES 250ML

A wonderfully bitter-sweet drink and perfect made into a cocktail with a splash of vodka, twist of lemon peel and topped up with carbonated water, or use in Rowan berry and star anise jellies (page 87).

INGREDIENTS

- 250g rowan berries
- 300ml water
- 100g golden granulated sugar

In a small saucepan, add the rowan berries and water, there should be enough to cover the berries.

Bring to the boil and simmer over a low heat for 30 minutes with the lid on. Strain through a jelly bag or fine muslin cloth into a medium sized bowl or measuring jug and leave to drip through for about 20 minutes.

Pour the liquid (there should be about 200-220ml) and sugar back into the rinsed saucepan, and stir over a medium heat until the sugar has dissolved.

While still warm, pour into a sterilised bottle and seal.

ROWAN BERRY AND STAR ANISE JELLIES

SERVES 4

These sophisticated flavoured jellies combine the complex flavour of rowan berries with the sweetness of star anise.

INGREDIENTS

* 4 leaves of gelatine
* 350ml water
* 4 star anise
* 150ml rowan berry cordial

Place the leaves of gelatine in cold water for 5-10 minutes or until soft, then squeeze out the excess water.

Meanwhile, bring the water and the star anise to the boil in a medium, lidded pan. Simmer for 5 minutes before adding the cordial and bring to just steaming. Remove from the heat and stir in the gelatine leaves until they dissolve.

At this stage you can choose to place a star anise into each small ramekin dish or individual jelly mould or discard them. I like to keep them in the jellies as they are so visually pleasing and are nice to suck when you find them in the jelly (I don't recommend eating them though!).

Evenly distribute the liquid between 4 ramekin dishes or individual jelly moulds. Leave to cool for 3-4 hours. Eat alone or with cream.

SEA BEET/SPINACH
Beta vulgaris ssp. Maritima

Where	Coastal areas.
How abundant	Very, where found.
Edible parts	Leaves, roots (permission needed to dig up roots and they may be years old and very fibrous).
Season	Primarily spring, second growth in autumn/winter.
Nutritional/ medicinal	Rich in vitamin C and A and contains a range of minerals.

The mother and father of most cultivated beets, including some varieties of spinach, beetroot and sugar beet. Keeps its shape beautifully when cooked.

Get the ID right!
- Bright green leaves taper down into a ribbed stem; stem occasionally red-striped.
- Leaves are thick and glossy, and come into a spear shape.
- When flowering, can trail to up to 80cm in length, with tiny flowers that may be white, green or red/pink (bottom right photo).

Suggested recipes and uses
Use the same as cooked spinach; as a side vegetable, in risotto or seafood dishes. Best cooked, though the really young leaves can be used raw.

Tips
Wilts down just like spinach, despite its sometimes tough exterior. Some prefer to remove the main stalk, and just use the tender parts. I like to use it whole.

SEA SPINACH WITH PAN-FRIED SEA BASS AND SORREL BUTTER

SERVES 4

A fresh-from-the-sea dish with the unadulterated flavours of sea beet, line-caught sea bass and wild flavoured, lemony sorrel butter. Serve as small dish or as a main meal with buttered potatoes.

INGREDIENTS

- 1 tbsp vegetable oil
- 5 tbsp sorrel butter (page 102)
- 4 fillets of white, sustainable fish, such as sea bass
- freshly ground black pepper
- 200g sea spinach leaves

Add the vegetable oil and one tablespoon of the sorrel butter into a frying pan over a medium heat.

When the butter is melted and the oil is hot, add the fillets of fish and sprinkle with black pepper. Cook for about 3 minutes on each side or until cooked through, using a fish slice to turn over.

The fish is cooked when it falls apart easily with no pink flesh, be careful not to overcook.

Simultaneously cook the sea spinach leaves in a small pan in a small amount of water for about 3 minutes or until tender.

Serve hot and together with the fish with dots of sorrel butter on the fish and spinach.

SEA RADISH
Raphanus raphanistrum ssp. Maritimus

Where	Sandy soil near the coast.
How abundant	Very, in undisturbed areas.
Edible parts	Leaves, flowers, young seed pods.
Season	Leaves in spring and autumn, flower and seed pods in summer.
Nutritional/ medicinal	Little known, though cultivated radishes contain good levels of copper, manganese, potassium, vitamin C and some calcium, magnesium, iron and zinc. Anti-bacterial and anti-fungal properties and used for coughs, respiratory and digestive issues.

Another member of the cabbage (brassica family). There's a wonderful heat to the leaves and seed pods of this original, wild radish. The flavour will remind you of the round, red salad roots we know as radishes even if the look of the plant confuses you! The flowers are a little more subtle.

Get the ID right!
- Grows up to 1 metre tall.
- Hairy plant, with rough lower leaves, grows in a rosette form at ground level, before becoming upright.
- Leaves have ragged, toothed edges, that wave in and out from the stem, with smaller leaflets lower on the stem.
- Stems, thick and juicy, flowers pale yellow, four petals (brassica/cabbage family) as with hedge mustard and hairy bittercress.
- Bulbous seed pods, like beads.

Suggested recipes and uses
Leaves fresh in pesto (use immediately), stems in stir fries, flowers raw in salads and garnishes. Leaves fried or raw (WFF in C&IOS, page 82). Seed pods raw as a snack, in salads or pickled.

Tips
Only eat seed pods when young, otherwise they become too fibrous. Cooking this plant removes some of the heat and can turn it into cabbage!

FRESH TOMATO SALSA WITH SEA RADISH LEAVES

SERVES 6-8 AS A SIDE DISH

A refreshing salad with the fiery flavours of red onion and fresh sea radish leaves.

INGREDIENTS

- 650g/4-6 fresh tomatoes
- 50g/handful of sea radish leaves
- ½ red onion
- ½ lime, juiced
- 1 dessertspoon white wine or rice vinegar

Chop the tomatoes and sea radish leaves, finely chop the onion and add together with the lime juice and vinegar.

Stir well and serve alongside steak, fish, chicken, tacos, nachos, burritos or quesadillas.

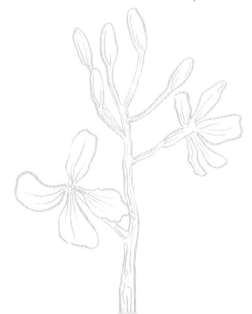

COMMON SORREL

Rumex acetosa

Where	Fields, grassland, hedgerows.
How abundant	Very, where found.
Edible parts	Leaves and young stems.
Season	Spring and then again in autumn.
Nutritional/ medicinal	High in vitamin C, contains plenty of vitamin A, plus B complex, E and K. Large levels of oxalic acid which can aggravate kidney stones and arthritis, as well as inhibit the absorption of other valuable minerals.

A wonderful lemony tang, some find the taste similar to apple peel. A definite favourite for many, and easy to spot everywhere, once you get your eye in.

Get the ID right!
- Grows up to 60cm in height.
- Arrow-shaped leaves that come down into a point (always to a sharp point), either side of the stem.
- Stem is channelled (U-shaped).
- Sometimes with red markings on the leaves, or pinkish at the base of the stem.
- Flowers are reddish or green (top right photo), like small discs, in bunches on stems.

Suggested recipes and uses
Raw in salads, great in a yoghurt dip and traditional sorrel soup (WFF in C&IOS, page 90) flash cook in omelettes, or in a white sauce with fish. Can make a good sorbet or ice-cream (W&S).

Tips
Use irregularly and in conjunction with milk, yoghurt or cheese to counter the binding up of calcium (see nutritional/medicinal). Cooking also considerably reduces the oxalic acid content.

WOOD SORREL
Oxalis acetosella

Where	Woods, hedgerows, banks, shady areas.
How abundant	Very, where found.
Edible parts	Leaves and stems.
Season	Throughout the year, best in spring.
Nutritional/ medicinal	Rich in vitamin C and contains flavonoids and beta-carotene. Contains oxalic acid which should not be eaten in large amounts (see page 96 on Common Sorrel).

A delicate leaf from the wood sorrel family which make beautiful, edible decorations that share the citrusy flavour of common sorrel.

Get the ID right!
- Grows to 10cm tall.
- Leaves are trefoil, with 3 heart-shaped parts which close down into a pyramid shape at night or in a lot of shade.
- White flowers with 5 petals and often mauve vein.
- Can cover large areas of ground.

Suggested recipes and uses
Similar to common sorrel for suggestions, though haven't shared specific recipes for wood sorrel as it is small and works perfectly as an edible decoration.

Tips
Use scissors to cut. Do not consume too much due to oxalic acid content (page 96).

CRUST-LESS SORREL QUICHE

SERVES 6-8

An easy to make, softly textured dish which is something between a quiche and a frittata. Serve with salads, potatoes or grains.

INGREDIENTS

- 10 free-range eggs
- 250ml milk
- 50g sorrel leaves
- 20g wild garlic leaves
- salt and pepper (to taste)

Preheat the oven to 180°C/fan 160°C/350°F/gas mark 4.

Line a 20cm x 20cm baking tin with baking parchment. Just scrunch or fold it down at the corners.

In a large bowl or jug whisk together the eggs and milk. Roughly chop the sorrel and garlic leaves and add in along with the salt and pepper, to tatse.

Pour into the lined tin and bake for 30-35 minutes, or until set and slightly golden.

Leave to cool for 10 minutes before slicing.

SORREL BUTTER

MAKES ABOUT 8 SERVINGS

I love the tart flavour of sorrel in this wild, herb butter. Beautiful melted on freshly cooked fish, or hot baked potatoes or on wilted sea spinach (page 90).

INGREDIENTS

- 2 tbsp washed and dried, fresh sorrel leaves
- 120g butter, room temperature

Finely chop the sorrel leaves and place in a medium sized bowl along with the butter and blend together with a fork or spoon. Keep in the fridge and use within 5 days or roll into a long sausage shape, wrap in greaseproof paper and freeze. You can then slice off chunks as and when needed.

SORREL DIP

SERVES 4

A really simple, zingy dip. Enjoy with crusty bread, veggie or bread sticks. Great as an alternative to raita alongside curry or instead of tzatziki with warm pitta bread and lamb.

INGREDIENTS

- 250g natural, full-fat yoghurt
- 45g sorrel leaves
- 1 tbsp virgin olive oil
- salt and pepper (to taste)

Blend the ingredients together. Taste, adjust and serve.

Keeps well for 5 days in the fridge.

ABOUT THE AUTHOR

Rachel Lambert has been teaching foraging since 2007 and is an award-winning author on foraging and cooking. She has previously written and created photographs for *Wild Food Foraging in Cornwall and the Isles of Scilly* and *Seaweed Foraging in Cornwall and the Isles of Scilly*, both published by Tor Mark Ltd. In 2022 she published Wild and Sweet – Forage and Make 101 Seasonal Desserts through Hoxton Mini Press. Rachel has made her home in Penzance, West Cornwall, she lived and studied in Devon in the 1990s. Find out more about her courses, blogs and books at www.wildwalks-southwest.co.uk.

ACKNOWLEDGEMENTS

Thanks to Anna at Tor Mark Ltd for asking me to write this book, to Briony and the rest of the Tor Mark team for all your hard work. Thank you for Mandy and Martin for that enlightening walk all those decades ago. Thanks to all those who've come on my foraging walks, courses and events – your questions, sharing and company have been invaluable. Thank you to nature herself for all her infinite wisdom and giving, to the plants for their nutrition and medicine. Thank you Elliott White, and Tom Bailey for sharing your photographs.